Dedi

Table of Contents

Table of Contents Cont.

My Beloved Daughter,

My love for you is unconditional. You will never have to do anything to earn My love and affection because you are my treasured daughter. You are "Daddy's Girl." How My heart breaks for you when I see you seek others to find the love that only I can give. I know how hard it is for you when you cannot see Me in the natural because you're looking for My love in a person.

I am a very personal God that meets you in places that no one else can because I am the One that created you. If you would seek Me the way you seek others to feel loved, you will realize that even though you can't see Me yet, you will feel me. My deepest desire is for you to experience My love for you, so deeply that you would never doubt or feel desperate for love again. But I will not force My way into your heart. I will wait patiently for you to invite Me in, and when you're ready, we will walk together as Father and daughter everyday for the rest of your life—until the day I see your precious face in heaven.

Love,
Your Heavenly Father Who Adores You

"I have loved you with an everlasting love; therefore I have continued my faithfulness to you."
Jeremiah 31:3

Royal Reflection

How you feel about yourself will never change the way your Heavenly Father feels about you.

Royal Reflection

Royal Reflection

My Princess,

You are royalty even when you don't feel like a princess.
How you feel about yourself will never change the fact
that you are a part of My royal family, My daughter. I am
the King of Kings which means you are royalty.
I know you struggle to see yourself for who you really are,
but don't allow your insecurities to keep you from stepping
out in faith and believing that you could make a
difference. I believe in you even when you don't believe in
yourself. I know you don't know where to start or how to
become what I've called you to be.

You can start by recognizing who I am, the King of
Kings and your Daddy in Heaven. If you will make Me the
reason you live, everything you do will come to life,
including your passion for the things that matter most to
Me. You are called to be a beautiful light in this dark
world, but only you can choose to step into your royal
calling and represent Me. This is your time, My beloved, to
take your appointed position in the royal family. Others
will see the love in your eyes and compassion in your heart
and it will draw them to Me, because I am in you. Never
try to fit in again. You were born to stand out to lead those
who are lost to have eternal life in my   kingdom…Your
future home!

Love,
Your King Who Chose You

"But you are a chosen race, a royal priesthood, a holy
nation, a people for his own possession, that you may
proclaim the excellences of him who called
you out of darkness into his marvelous light."
1 Peter 2:9

Royal Reflection

God's presence is permanent but His promises are personal, and they depend on how much you compromise or commit to your Royal Call.

Royal Reflection

Royal Reflection

The Power of Prayers

My Warrior Daughter,

You have My full attention when you call My name. Don't ever underestimate the power of your prayers. I want you to confidently call on heaven so that you may see My mighty hand move on earth. Your words spoken in someone's dark hour will move My Spirit to light their path. Your prayer for someone who is lonely will usher in My comfort. Your prayer for protection over someone in danger will send My angels to their aid.

There is an invisible war around you, and your prayers are the evidence of My power at work in the world. One day, on the other side of eternity, you will see how your prayers affected and protected many lives while you lived.

Love,
Your God Who Loves When You Pray

"And I will do whatever you ask in my name,
so that the Son may bring glory to the Father.
You may ask me for anything in
my name, and I will do it."
John 14:13-14

Royal Reflection

Know the power you hold in being Chosen of the Most High. You have been given the ear of the King of kings!

Royal Reflection

Royal Reflection

My Daughter,

Faith is the only thing that will hold you together when the world around you seems to be falling apart. I want you to learn to live your life fueled by faith; there is nothing too big for Me to handle for you, My beloved. I am your God who will move a mountain if it stands in the way of My will for you.

My power will be seen in your circumstance when you begin to believe I am who I say I am, and I will do as I promise. You are Mine and I hold in My hand all you will ever need. I love you, but I cannot force you to live by faith. It is your choice. Only you can make the decision to believe and experience the mighty works I want you to see.

Love,
Your King Who Has Faith In You

"What is faith? It is the confident assurance that what we hope for is going to happen. It is the evidence of things we cannot yet see."
Hebrews 11:1

Royal Reflection

*May you never forget all the times your Savior
pulled you through the darkness in the past.*

Royal Reflection

Royal Reflection

Keys To Your Freedom

My Daughter,

I have walked with you all the days of your life. I've seen your past and I know your future. I have so many plans I want to walk out with you, but as long as you're looking back, we cannot move forward together. I will stand by you, even if you choose to stand still the rest of your life. But if you will accept My gift of a new beginning, you will find the new life your heart and soul long for.

Looking in a rearview mirror will only remind you of all that has gone wrong. If you choose to let go of what's behind you and fix your eyes on what's in front of you, I will be able to move you into a future filled with faith adventures. It's time to trust Me when I say, "There's nothing you have done, or that anyone has done to you, that must keep you chained to your past." I sent My Son, Jesus, your Savior, to break every chain so you could be free. Only you can choose to walk out of the prison of your past and walk into the hope of a new future. I am here outside the door of your heart patiently waiting for you to let Me unlock you from the chains that are too heavy for you to cast off. I sacrificed My son for you to be free, don't waste what I have given you... His name is Jesus, your Savior who loved you with His life.

Love,
Your King & Key to Freedom

"Anyone who belongs to Christ has become
a new person. The old life is gone;
a new life has begun!"
2 Corinthians 5:17

Royal Reflection

*It's time to leave your past where it belongs,
at the Cross.*

Royal Reflection

Royal Reflection

My Daughter,

You are never alone on the battlefield, My beloved warrior. I would never expect you to handle this life alone. That is why I sent My Holy Spirit to comfort you during combat. When you are overwhelmed by the spiritual warfare around you, I want you to call My name and I will come to your rescue.

I will destroy the works of the enemy and carry you to a place of restoration. I hear your heart from heaven and I will not waste a single tear that has fallen down your cheek. Your heart poured out to Me will cleanse your soul and joy will be yours once again!

Love,
Your King Who Wipes Away Your Tears

"He will once again fill your mouth with laughter and your lips with shouts of joy."
Job 8:21

Royal Reflection

Surrender your tears to heaven.
May you feel His mighty hand wipe your cheek
in the night and restore the
joy of your salvation!

Royal Reflection

Royal Reflection

My Daughter,

Every morning that you wake up is a new day. The old is gone and the new can be yours if you'll receive it. I want you to know there is never a wrong time to do the right thing. There is no choice wrong enough, there is no chain strong enough, and there is no time gone by long enough that can keep you from making things right in My sight. Now, there may be those who refuse to allow you to make things right, but their refusal to give you a chance to make things right does not keep Me from forgiving you. Yes, there will be consequences to wrong choices, and yes, I will discipline you because I love you.

I know how heavy it is to carry regret that is why I sent you a Savior to carry the weight of your sin to the cross. Now, My beloved, learn and let the mistakes make you wiser and the pain make you compassionate for those who do not know a new beginning is possible when I am invited to help turn a mess into a message of My mercy. Don't waste another day My beloved. Take me at My word. Live out My word to make the wrongs right, so you can move on with a clear and clean conscience from this day forward.

Love,
Your Faithful Father

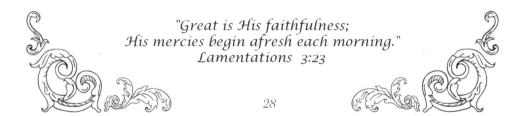

"Great is His faithfulness;
His mercies begin afresh each morning."
Lamentations 3:23

Royal Reflection

You will never regret doing the right thing.
There is never a wrong time to get right
with God and people.

Royal Reflection

Royal Reflection

You Can Trust Me

My Child,

I know how hard trust can be especially when you have experienced the heartache of loss. I understand because I Myself sacrificed My only son so you could be with Me for all eternity. With that said, I want you to let go and learn to trust Me with those you love.

I know your heart, and I know how much you love those close to you. I have given you loved ones to share your life with. But you, My child, must remember that those you love ultimately belong to Me—not to you. I didn't give you those relationships to tear you apart or to control you through fear of the future. I know how hard it is for you to trust Me when it appears I'm absent when you cry out to me. You must remember that each of your loved ones mean more to Me than they do to you. My plan may not always align with your prayer. My ways are higher than yours and I have the bigger picture that goes far beyond this life. Like Abraham did with his only son, Isaac, I am asking you to lay down those you love. Pray for peace, pray for comfort, pray for my kingdom purpose to come to pass in their life. It's time to free yourself from letting go of what you cannot control. Trust Me with everything that concerns you regarding them. Place your hand in Mine, and I promise I will walk you, and your loved ones, through all the things this life will bring until I bring you home.

Love,
Your Trustworthy King

"Those who trust in the Lord are secure as Mount Zion; they will not be defeated but will endure forever."
Psalm 125:1

Royal Reflection

Sometimes we pray so hard for what we want for our loved ones, we forget to pray His will for them.

Royal Reflection

Royal Reflection

Meet Me At The Alter

My Beloved,

I want to set you free from holding on to anyone but Me. Because I love you, I am asking you today to trust Me with those you love by laying them down at My altar. If you will obey Me, I will bless you as I blessed Abraham for laying down his much-loved son on the altar.

Remember, those I place in your life ultimately belong to Me. I know what is best because I created each of you. This test of your faith is not for Me, My beloved warrior . . . it is for you. I want you to walk the rest of your days in complete freedom and not fear for those you love!

Love,
Your King Who Is To Be Trusted

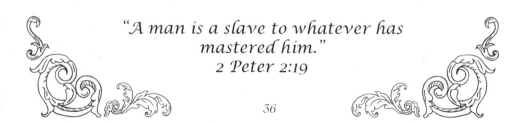

"A man is a slave to whatever has mastered him."
2 Peter 2:19

Royal Reflection

A praise song without a true heart behind it will never touch the human soul.

Royal Reflection

Royal Reflection

My Sweet Princess,

Your life is a sweet symphony that I Myself am composing note by note. I take your failures, your tears, your triumphs and your talents and I turn them into a glorious harmony that will be sung in the heavens for all eternity. All your thoughts and deeds are laid before Me like notes on a page. Every choice you make is a significant chord in an eternal arrangement. Don't let the noise of the world distract you from my magnificent melody, My beloved.

Seek Me in the quiet stillness of the morning, and I will fill your heart with divine music. Stay in rhythm with My Spirit throughout the day, and I will make your life an irresistible medley that will linger like sweet perfume in the hearts of all who journey with you. Walk with Me in absolute surrender, and you will draw others to Me in a rhapsody of praise. I want you, My girl, to praise your way through any and all things. Walk through them because you do not walk alone. I am here as a proud Papa looking for your beautiful praise song to fill the air!

Love,
Your King and Your Composer

"He has given me a new song to sing, a hymn of praise to our God.
Many will see what he has done and be astounded. They will put their trust in the Lord."
Psalm 40:3

Royal Reflection

Let the Lord be your love above all others.
May you find your security as you trust your
Lord by giving back to Him those
who are already His.

Royal Reflection

Royal Reflection

Courage To Change

My Brave Daughter,

I gave My life at the cross for you to have a better life, My beloved. But only you can make the choice to become all I have called you to be. Nothing will change without your effort and obedience to My word.

Your choice to let go of your old life and cling to the new life I offer will become the key to your freedom. You will find something far greater than temporary pleasure; you will find everlasting joy, unshakable peace, and renewed passion. This change will not only affect you. It will also make an everlasting impact on those you love.

Love,
Your King and Your Courage

"Therefore if anyone is in Christ,
he is a new creature; the old things passed away;
behold, new things have come."
2 Corinthians 5:17

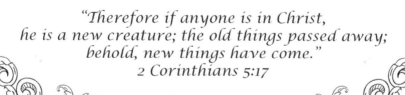

Royal Reflection

*Be compelled by His goodness and walk into the life
that He has for you, which is full of peace
and joy, redeeming love, and His
restoring power.*

Royal Reflection

Royal Reflection

My Daughter,

Not every open door in your life is from Me. If I opened the door, it will not cause you confusion. It will lead you to a closer relationship with Me. Don't immediately follow people through an open door simply because they claim to speak for Me, especially when they ask you to trust them more than Me and My Word. Don't seek counsel from those who don't walk in My wisdom or who don't live solely for Me. My open doors bring glory to My name and further My Kingdom. I am a God of order, and when I order your steps, I open doors that no man can shut.

So before you walk toward a new opportunity, be sure to pray and count the cost of what you are giving up. Take an honest look at where you will be going and whether you are headed in the most effective and everlasting direction. When you seek My guidance, you will hear My still voice say, "This is the way, My beloved, now walk in it."

Love,
Your Heavenly Father

""This is what the Lord says:Stop at the crossroads and look around. Ask for the old, godly way, and walk in it. Travel its path, and you will find rest for your souls."
Jeremiah 6:16

Royal Reflection

Before you walk through any door,
consider where it is leading you
and what it will cost you.

Royal Reflection

Royal Reflection

Hopelessness Is An Illusion

My Daughter,

Hopelessness is just an illusion, My beloved warrior. I am your hope and your future is in My hands. Just as I parted the Red Sea of hopelessness for Moses and My chosen people, I will part your sea and you will walk in the promises I have for your life. Don't allow the illusion of the enemy to become reality. Fires will never burn you out; raging waters will not drown your dreams. I am bigger than any challenge you are facing.

Now, My Princess Warrior, fight the temptation to give up and allow Me to walk you into a life filled with indescribable hope for your future!

Love,
Your King and Your Hope

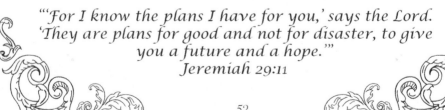

"'For I know the plans I have for you,' says the Lord. 'They are plans for good and not for disaster, to give you a future and a hope.'"
Jeremiah 29:11

Royal Reflection

No matter how bad your circumstances seem, may your heart will be filled with unshakable hope in your Lord and in your future.

Royal Reflection

Royal Reflection

I Can Heal Your Heart

My Beloved Girl,

I know you live in a world where many relationships come to a bitter end, but I am not man; I am your Your Heavenly Daddy. I am not the one who caused the hurt or broke your heart, but I am the only one who can heal it. I know that when you're hurting you are tempted to blame Me for the actions of man. The truth is, I gave you who I loved most, my son Jesus, your savior who has felt every pain that you have.

Instead of running away from me, run to Me first, above all others. I will never reject you no matter what you've done or what's been done to you. Call for My comfort in the dark hours of the night and we will walk this out together. I will teach you how to guard your heart for the future, because your heart is the most precious gift you have to give away and you must protect it. I'm asking you to stop giving away what someone does not want to receive. I don't want my daughter reaching out to those who reject you and Me. Stop or you will miss out on those hearts who are ready to receive My love through you and love you the way you deserve to be loved.Remember, you will never find that true love you long for until I hold the first place position in your heart and head. Today is the day to let your tears fall on my shoulders so I can wash away my daughters pain caused by a person. Let your tears fall on Me as long as it takes for your past to die, your hurt to heal, and your hope to be born again so you will walk in wisdom and love freely.

Love,
Your Daddy Who Feels & Heals

"The Lord is close to the brokenhearted;
he rescues those whose spirits are crushed."
Psalm 34:18

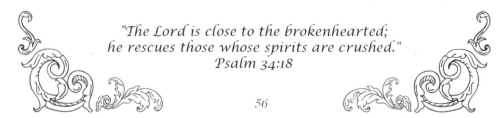

Royal Reflection

I wonder why we blame our Heavenly daddy for Satan's work, there's only one way for Satan to get back at God...Through His children that He loves.

Royal Reflection

Royal Reflection

My Daughter,

The enemy will always attempt to trap you by appealing to your earthly desires. His strategy has taken many of My chosen ones down into a pit of despair. Spiritual warfare is not a game, My Princess Warrior. It is very real, and you will have to run as far from temptation as you can to keep from falling prey to it.

I know running from the darkness may seem radical to many, but you are called to live a radical faith. I will always make a way of escape for you. But, you ultimately will make the choice to either bite the tempting bait of Satan or escape the snare of the enemy and run to Me.

Love,
Your King, The Great Escape

"God can be trusted not to let you be tempted too much, and he will show you how to escape from your temptations."
1 Corinthians 10:13

Royal Reflection

Always rely on your heavenly Father to be your
way of escape. May you cling to the one who
pushes through the dark forces
into the light.

Royal Reflection

Royal Reflection

My Warrior Princess,

I know the enemy can hit hard, but you are stronger than you think you are because My spirit is in you. This life will always have a problem to solve, a battle to fight, a storm to weather, a test to pass, a river of difficulty to walk through. "Through" is the key word to unlock your heart from fear and give you the faith to walk through anything. Your feelings will always deceive you, but my word will deliver you. Rise up, My princess warrior, and speak My word with courageous faith just as King David did as he stood up to Goliath; not with man-made armor, but with the shield of his faith in My powerful word. Just as I was with the future King David, I am with you, the Daughter of the king. Together, we are unbeatable. Your faith in Me to trust the outcome is critical as we will walk through this and all future battles together as Father and Daughter.

From this day forward, I want you to face forward with courageous faith in Me so you will experience My power personally and never doubt again. Every war you win in My strength will equip you for your calling, to live a life filled with extraordinary faith adventures and a living example for your loved ones to experience a faith-filled life!

Love,
Your King Who has Already Won

""The Lord is my strength, my shield from every danger. I trust in Him with all my heart.
He helps me, and my heart is filled with joy."
Psalm 28:7

Royal Reflection

If you put your faith in what you feel or see,
then you won't have the supernatural sight or
stamina necessary to keep your fight
and finish strong.

Royal Reflection

Royal Reflection

My Precious Warrior,

It is time to get dressed for battle, My beloved. You are more than my daughter; you are "My Princess Warrior". I called you to be at peace, but I've also called you to war. There are many who remain powerless and cannot fight for themselves, because they do not know Me. Yes, the fight to further My kingdom on earth will be fierce, because spiritual warfare is real, and the enemy wants to defeat you before you step out on the battlefield. However, you won't go alone. I am going with you to the front lines.

I will not let you be defenseless. In those times you feel as if there's no fight left inside of you, My Spirit will rise up inside your soul, and My strength will become your strength. My mighty armor will guard your heart from the fiery arrows of the enemy. In My power you will find your passion to face any spiritual giant that comes against your purpose. Hold your peace and focus on your purpose or you'll feel defeated. Remember this fight is not just for you; it's for all those who will watch you combat evil and conquer the enemy one soul at a time. In Me, your life will become the legacy of faith the next generation will need to stand on.

Love,
Your King who fights for you

"Therefore, put on every piece of God's armor so you will be able to resist the enemy in the time of evil. Then, after the battle, you will still be standing firm."
Ephesians 6:13

Royal Reflection

Why do we avoid the faith advantage of spiritual warfare when we know we win in the end? What good is all of the armor of God if there is no need to use it?

Royal Reflection

Royal Reflection

My Warrior Daughter,

I know that your identity is under a great attack every day as you are bombarded with lies of the enemy. Too many times I see you surrender by allowing Satan to make you feel worthless. Don't bow down to these man-made idols to find your worth. You are Mine, and this identity crisis is not My will for you, My beloved treasure.

Allow Me alone to appraise your true value and worth. I already proved to you how much you are worth on the cross at Calvary. Starting today, begin to embrace what you really are—My Treasured Possession and My Crown Jewel, chosen by Me, the King above all kings!

Love,
Your King Who Defines You

"But you are a chosen people, a royal priesthood, a holy nation, a people belonging to God, that you may declare the praises of him who called you out of darkness into his wonderful light."
1 Peter 2:9
Lamentations 3:23

Royal Reflection

May you never allow anyone to tell you who you are except for your Heavenly Father, who knows the real you.

Royal Reflection

Royal Reflection

My Timeless Princess,

I know that sometimes you look back on your life with anguish and regret--so much time wasted on things that did not matter. Take heart, My love. I am your Redeemer, and today is a new day. Your time is eternal because you will live forever in My kingdom. Your here and now on earth is equally important because there are many that need to know Me through you.

The enemy wants you to feel like time is wasted, but I want you to know what you've learned through all the good, the bad, the lost years are a part of the plan of preparing you for your purpose. So start now by letting go of yesterday and choosing to start today seeking Me with all your heart, your mind, and your strength. My plan for you does not have an expiration date. Just as I used the years of rejection, false accusations, and deep despair in Joseph's life to lead him to a position of leadership, influence, and blessing, I will also use your past experiences teach you and not torment you. Remember, my princess, I will always work something good out of what others meant for your harm.

If you will let go of what was done, what was said, and what you want, I will redeem what was lost If you will let Me.

Love,
Your King and your Redeemer

"'For I know the plans I have for you,'
Declares the Lord, 'Plans to prosper you and not to harm you, plans to give you hope and a future.'"
Jeremiah 29:11

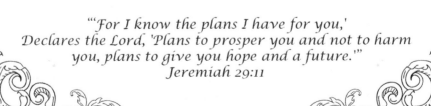

Royal Reflection

*You are already transformed by
His timeless love for you.*

Royal Reflection

Royal Reflection

My Warrior Daughter,

Don't engage in relational battles that drain your strength trying to prove your point, win your way, or defend yourself. I am your defense, and if you will fight the temptation to give in to relational battles, I will reward you with perfect peace.

You are called to live above a life of anger and bitterness. The truth is that nothing anyone has said or done to you can stop My perfect plans or promises from coming to pass in your life. Now break through to a life filled with peace by walking away from the relational wars of wrath. It is time to fight for the things worth fighting for, and win souls for My kingdom!

Love,
Your King Who Is Your Defense

"Do not take revenge, my friends, but leave room for God's wrath, for it is written: 'It is mine to avenge; I will repay,' says the Lord."
Romans 12:19

Royal Reflection

God will give you the wisdom to navigate through relational traps set by the enemy to distract you.

Royal Reflection

Royal Reflection

Beautifully Broken

My Beloved Daughter,

What you may see as broken inside yourself, I see as beautiful. I am the One who makes beautiful things out of broken hearts. I am the same God who took a brokenhearted orphan named Esther and turned her into a queen who saved My people. Just as I used Esther's pain for My will, I will not waste a single tear you have shed, My love.

I can and will use whatever is broken in your life for My glory. My love and mercy will shine brightest in those broken places. I will not only use what is broken, I will rebuild you to become even better and more beautiful than you could ever imagine.

Love,
Your King Who Sees Your True Beauty

"Yet God has made everything beautiful for its own time. He has planted eternity in the human heart, but even so, people cannot see the whole scope of God's work from beginning to end."
Ecclesiastes 3:11

Royal Reflection

*Bring your brokenness to God so that He can turn
you into something more beautiful than
you could ever be on your own.*

Royal Reflection

Royal Reflection

My Royal Runner,

I know life can become exhausting and hard to stay on track, but now is not the time to quit running. I am your life coach and you will find the strength to run your race in My Word. With my coaching you will not only run steadfast, you will win many souls for My Kingdom along the way. I don't want you to waste your race by running for the praises of people which will make you become weak and weary. You have been designed by Me to win a royal race that is only yours and no one else's. If you will throw aside every weight that slows you down. I will empower you will run in the freedom and power that has been given to you by My son's great sacrifice. You, My princess, must run with blinders on by keeping your eyes fixed on the eternal prize. You are more than a conqueror in Jesus, You are destined to win!

Your amazing faith race will be rewarded with a crown that will never fade and will forever be remembered by all who watched you finish strong!

Love,
Your Lord and Life Coach

"Don't you realize that in a race everyone runs, but only one person gets the prize? So run to win! All athletes are disciplined in their training.
They do it to win a prize that will fade away, but we do it for an eternal prize."
1 Corinthians 9:24-25

Royal Reflection

What good is it running for the praises of people if we win no souls for the kingdom of God?

Royal Reflection

Royal Reflection

My Prayer Princess,

You have My full attention when you call My name. Don't ever underestimate the power of your prayers. I want you to confidently call on heaven, that you may see My mighty hand move on earth. Your words spoken in someone's dark hour will move My Spirit to light their path. Your prayer for someone who is lonely will usher in My comfort. Your prayer for protection over someone in danger will send My angels to their aid. There is an invisible war around you and your prayers are the evidence of My power at work in the world.

Child of Mine, I want you to hold with great value that you have access to My throne, that you have been given My ear, and that I am the King of Kings! As my daughter, you can ask me anything according to my perfect will for your life and I will answer. It may not be the answer you want, but your prayers move My hand from heaven and give you a greater answer, my ultimate answer that will put you in your purpose and change the lives of those you pray for forever. My Spirit lives in you and your prayers surrendered to my answer will make us an unstoppable force of light in these dark times.

One day, on the other side of eternity, you will see how your prayers effected and protected many lives while you lived.

Love,
Your God who loves when you pray

"Then if my people who are called by my name will humble themselves and pray and seek my face and turn from their wicked ways, I will hear from heaven and will forgive their sins and restore their land."
2 Chronicles 7:14

Royal Reflection

You have been given the ear of the King of Kings and personal access to His private throne room, because you are His daughter.

Royal Reflection

Royal Reflection

My Daughter,

The only thing that's going to matter when this life is over is the time you invest in the things that last in My kingdom. Remember that you are "Royalty." The time I give you in this life is extremely valuable and I am asking you to set strict boundaries so you don't waste My gift of life. Hear Me when I say that it's okay to say no to others so you can say yes to Me!

Let Me help you take control of your commitments by presenting them to Me in prayer. I would never ask you to overextend yourself, but others will because they don't understand the value of your time. Come t o Me when you feel out of control and overextended. I will take you to a place where you can be still and we can reason and reflect on others wants and My will for this season of your life. I don't want My daughter to allow others demands or the demands you place on yourself to overrule My command for your time to rest and refresh. Even My son, Jesus, needed to walk away from the demands of the crowd and find time alone with Me. It's time to bless yourself with new boundaries, so you can begin to breathe, preserve your peace of mind, and allow yourself to live on purpose.

Love,
Your King of Time

"Mark out a straight path for your feet; then stick to the path and stay safe. Don't get sidetracked."
Proverbs 4:26

Royal Reflection

*Boundaries are a blessing that will become
your guard, your gauge, and
your guide for life.*

Royal Reflection

Royal Reflection

My Warrior Daughter,

I am never too tired to carry you when you're too weak to walk. This is one of the privileges of being My Princess. Take my gift of a Sabbath and rest, My beloved. Allow your body and mind to refuel while you rest. I am the One who wants to bear all burdens.

Now, rest in Me to receive My perfect peace, which will refresh and renew your strength.

Let go and find rest for your weary soul.

Love,
Your God Of Perfect Peace

"Come to me all who are weary and heavy burdens and I will give you rest.
Take my yoke upon you and learn from me and you will find rest for your soul."
Matthew 11:28-29

Royal Reflection

Find peace in knowing your God has you covered
and wants the chance to care for you,
so you can breathe in any
battle you may face.

Royal Reflection

Royal Reflection

My Beloved Daughter,

I want to help you discern the difference between a human push and the Holy Spirit pull. I will never push you into anything, so I'm asking you to pay attention when you feel pressured, panicked, or pushed by someone or something; because those feelings are never from Me. I am a loving father that will lead you with a peaceful pull of my Holy Spirit, so pay attention to what is pushing you out of My will and out of the way of where you want to be with Me. When I lead my children, the Israelites, out of slavery in Egypt, I closed the sea behind them so they would never feel pushed again to go back to the place from which I delivered them. Remember, I want to bring you into a place of promise for your life while the enemy wants to bring you to a place of pain, punishment, and push you out of your purpose.

I make a way to enter into excellence while the enemy will make a way to entangle you. Whenever you feel paralyzed, pushed, or panicked, don't follow those feelings because they will lead you where you don't want to go. Take time instead to pray, get perspective, and wait for My leading of peace and My pull on your heart to move you into a greater position than you could ever imagine.

Love,
Your Heavenly Father

"And your ears shall hear a word behind you, saying, "This is the way, walk in it," when you turn to the right or when you turn to the left."
Isaiah 30:21

Royal Reflection

God would never lead us to a place where we have no purpose or peace, and the pressure of person is not a pull of the Holy Spirit.

Royal Reflection

Royal Reflection

My Warrior Daughter,

I called you My Princess, and with that calling comes a responsibility to purify yourself. I have set you apart and given you a new life. You can help conquer the corruption around you by making your life a true reflection of My standards. I am not asking for perfection, My beloved, but I am asking for your purity to be a priority. I am requesting that you remove from your path anything that causes you to fall away from Me.

It is your purity that will bring My promises to pass in your life. It is purity that gives you the power to effectively proclaim you are Mine!

Love,
Your King Who Purifies You

"Purify yourself for the Lord is getting ready to do great and mighty things among you."
Joshua 3:5

Royal Reflection

*Purify yourself for the Lord so you can experience
a greater joy that any impure pleasure. I pray
your purity brings great change to those
God has given you influence.*

Royal Reflection

Royal Reflection

My Beloved Daughter,

As your father, I want you to understand the gift of grace that I have given you so you don't have the pressure to be perfect or to perform for Me or for anyone else. It's important that you understand that when you choose to disobey Me, grace does not stop the consequences of sin, but it does give you a deeper understanding of why the cross had to happen.

It isn't until you come to a place where you know you need a savior, that grace can give you a glimpse of My goodness and My unconditional love for you. Grace gives you glimpse of how I can use every good and bad choice that you will ever make to do something that will prove My grace.

Grace is your guarantee that I can work and will work all things together for your good if you will allow Me to display My divinity in your humanity. With that said, I love you just as much when you're sinning as when you are completely committed to me. So I'm asking you to never allow what you've done or said to keep you from coming to Me to receive the gift of grace that I want to give you every new day until I return for you.

Love,
Your Heavenly Father

"Well then, should we keep on sinning so that God can show us more and more of his wonderful grace?"
Romans 6:1

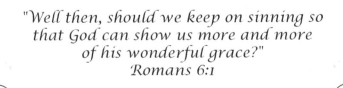

Royal Reflection

Grace is a treasure, so we need to be careful not to use it to trash our lives or loved ones.

Royal Reflection

Royal Reflection

My Daughter,

I will not waste your pain, My beloved. I will use every tear you have cried to put a passion in your heart to do something great for My Kingdom. You can find comfort in your darkest hour by praising Me through the painful place you're in. You will not remain in this painful place for long, My love.

Soon you will see that I carved something in your character through it all that will draw you and others closer to Me. You are my precious princess and I will shake the earth if that is what it takes to see your chains fall to the ground.

Love,
Your Lord Who Feels Your Pain

"Paul and Silas were praying and singing hymns to God, and the other prisoners were listening. Suddenly, there was a great earthquake and all the doors flew open, and the chains of every prisoner fell off!"
Acts 16:25-26

Royal Reflection

As you praise Him through your pain, you will feel Him unlock the chains. May you discover for yourself His divine deliverance from depression and hopelessness.

Royal Reflection

Royal Reflection

My Warrior Daughter,

It's time, My warrior, to surrender your fears, your insecurities, your pain, and your loved ones completely to Me. I want your whole heart and mind and soul to be worry-free. I want your complete trust so you can focus on your faith and be free of the spirit of fear.

Give up the fight of trying to figure it all out. Don't let your circumstances hold your heart hostage or cause you to lose your confidence in Me. I am asking you on this day to answer this one question: In whom do you place your trust?

Love,
Your Trustworthy King

"But those who trust in the Lord will find new strength. They will soar high on wings like eagles. They will run and not grow weary They will walk and not faint."
Isaiah 40:31

Royal Reflection

Lay down and let go of whatever is holding you hostage to worry and fear. It's time surrender to the sweet peace that comes when you choose to trust your Heavenly Father.

Royal Reflection

Royal Reflection

My Beloved Daughter,

Today I am asking you to search your heart and ask this question: "Whom do you seek for approval?" Are you living your life for the approval and praise of people, or Me? I want to save you from exhausting yourself by performing for a world that does not want to praise you. I designed you to desire only Me, and Me alone. When you choose to live for Me, you will never again be thirsty for attention, because you will be hydrated in My love and adoration for you.

Now let Me ask you again, My beloved daughter: "Whose praise do you seek?"

Love,
Your King Who Seeks After You

"Am I now trying to win the approval of men, or of God? Or am I trying to please men? If I were still trying to please men, I would not be a servant of Christ."
Galatians 1:10

Royal Reflection

*Know that your heavenly Father adores you and loves
to shower you with praise. May you be forever free
from the bondage of needing the praises of people,
knowing how valuable you are
to your God!*

Royal Reflection

Royal Reflection

My Beloved Daughter,

I created you and I know exactly what you need, but only you can decide if you will allow yourself to obey what I know is best for My daughter. I have given you a command to rest that, as your father, I'm expecting you to obey for your own good. My command for you to rest is not just for Me, it is for you. The enemy wants to wear you out because he knows rest is your weapon for warfare. Yes, spiritual warfare is real and if you are exhausted you will not have the stamina to sustain. I want you to understand that rest is not just sleeping. Resting in Me is just as important for your peace of mind and your perseverance as physical rest. I will never ask you to do anything that would keep you from being still with Me or keep you from sleeping. The enemy knows he cannot steal you from Me, which is why he wants to steal every day from you. Because you are part of My royal family and your body is where my Holy Spirit dwells. So when you feel guilty for giving yourself the gift of rest, remember that you're not just stealing a night sleep from yourself, you are stealing it from the place where My spirit dwells. I want you to know that I love you and I would never give you anything that causes you exhaustion. What I give you to do I give you the grace to do. If you will rest, you will experience exhilaration and the excitement of having a clear mind and a rested body. It's time to give in to your wants and your need to be still and to rest so you're restless spirit can come to a place of perfect peace.

Turn off whatever is taking away your time to rest because you deserve it, my daughter, and it is My delight to see you refreshed from rest!

Love,
Your Heavenly Father

"My presence shall go with you, and I will give you rest.
I lay down and slept; I awoke, for the LORD sustains me.
In peace I will both lie down and sleep."
Psalm 4:8

Royal Reflection

What good are all the blessings of God,
if we are too exhausted to enjoy them?

Royal Reflection

Royal Reflection

My Daughter,

I know sometimes you feel afraid to be real with me, But I am your Heavenly Father and what I want most from you as my daughter is a very real relationship with you. I want you to know that you don't ever have to pretend with Me because I am your safe place. I am not expecting you to pretend pain is not real, but I cannot hear what you will not reveal and I cannot fix what you fake, My beloved. I am here and wanting you to share your real struggles. I am asking you to take a step close to Me, your daddy in heaven that loves and adores you.

I would never expect you to be strong in your own strength, that's why I give you My strength, the Holy Spirit in you. I am your freedom from falsehood. I know the real you, however, I want to help you know the real you. Anything that does not have a foundation of truth, including your feelings, will fail you every time. Don't listen when the enemy of your soul whispers that you can save yourself from the pain and problems of this world. When something hurts you or someone angers you, tell Me how you really feel so we can reason together.

Love,
Your Heavenly Father

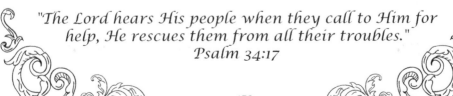

"The Lord hears His people when they call to Him for help, He rescues them from all their troubles."
Psalm 34:17

Royal Reflection

*Many times we wonder why we feel that God
is not real, maybe it's because we are
not real with Him.*

Royal Reflection

Royal Reflection

My Princess,

I know how hard it is for you to believe when you walk by sight and not by faith. But the one thing I desire is for you to believe that I am who I say I am. Faith isn't getting what you want my love, faith isn't something you say, it's something you know. Faith in me is the only thing that will hold you together when your world seems to be falling apart. If you have to see to believe, you will never experience the exhilaration of walking by faith.

The most exciting thing about being in the royal family is that have the privilege of knowing, without seeing and believing before a promise comes to pass.

I want my daughter to be so secure in Me that you will not be shaken by any doubts, insecurities, or trials that the enemy tries to throw at you. I am your God who will move a mountain if it stands in the way of My will for you. My power will be seen in your circumstance when you begin to believe. You are Mine, but I cannot force you to live by faith, it is your choice. I long for your faith to be increased to the point that you never again forget all the times in the past that I faithfully pulled you through, knowing I will do it again.

Love,
Your King Who Has Faith in You

"He replied, 'Because you have so little faith. I tell you the truth, if you have faith as small as a mustard seed, you can say to this mountain, 'Move from here to there' and it will move. Nothing will be impossible for you."
Matthew 17:20-21

Royal Reflection

Thinking about Jesus and Judas could cause us to lose faith. However, Judas's betrayal got Jesus to what he came to do for us.

Royal Reflection

Royal Reflection

My Daughter,

My words spoken through you change the atmosphere around you.   Today and everyday you have a choice to make; you can speak life to yourself and to others, or you can speak death. Your tongue is a powerful weapon and with it you build others up or tear them down. You can speak with compassion, or you can crush someone's spirit.

I want you, My beloved, to use your words to counteract the enemy's verbal attacks on My people. Ask Me to anoint your lips to speak life, and you will bring hope to the hopeless and life-changing truth to those lost in lies. Let me control your tongue and your words that bring healing and hope to all who hear them. Your lips will speak the truth and bring a refreshing word every time you open your mouth to speak.

Pray and prepare your heart so your words will be like a sweet aroma that fills every room you walk in.

Love,
Your Heavenly Father

"Lord Take control of what I say, O Lord, and guard my lips."
Psalm 141:3

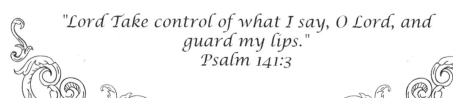

Royal Reflection

Better that you would quietly allow God to get you through uncomfortable situations than pay the price of saying something you later regret.

Royal Reflection

Royal Reflection

My Princess,

I want you to truly know that nothing is impossible with Me if you are faithful. I will use you to do things that you could never imagine, if you will take the first step toward greatness by giving Me everything that holds you back or compromises your royal calling. Never forget, you have My Spirit inside of you. Therefore, you have

My power to live a life without limits. There is no mountain big enough that I cannot move. There is no problem hard enough that I cannot solve. There is no heart broken enough that I cannot heal. There are no chains strong enough that I cannot break. Nothing can keep you back from My blessings but your disobedience or lack of faith. Now, step out on the water where real faith advantage and adventures begin by choosing to live by my commands—and watch Me open the windows of heaven for you. It's time to surrender your dreams and give Me the chance to do immeasurably more than you would ever dare ask of Me or imagine.

Love,
Your King Who Knows

"Now to him who is able to do immeasurably more than all we ask or imagine, according to his power that is at work within us."
Ephesians 3:20

Royal Reflection

*Let us never put God in a box, instead let's
allow Him to be a surprise gift
we were not expecting.*

Royal Reflection

Royal Reflection

God Confidence

My Warrior Daughter,

I am asking you today to surrender your confidence to Me. Don't give the power to build your self-confidence to other people. This world has nothing to offer you that will build you up and keep you strong when times get tough. I am the only One who can water your thirsty soul and give you assurance about who you are.

I want you, My beloved warrior, to walk in the confidence that cannot be taken or shaken by anyone or any circumstance. Now is the time to trade your insecurities for security in Me. Together, we will be unstoppable and conquer much during your life!

Love,
Your King and Your Confidence

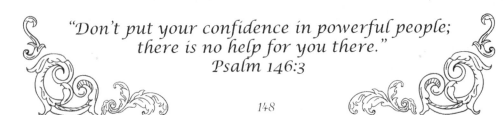

"Don't put your confidence in powerful people; there is no help for you there."
Psalm 146:3

Royal Reflection

May you knock down the lies the enemy has told you and walk confident and secure in your calling.

Royal Reflection

Royal Reflection

My Dear Daughter,

Love is not a game; It is a gift. If anyone is playing games with your heart to get their way with you, I'm asking you to trust Me and walk away. I want my daughter to be free from the power of people. I want you to understand what true love is, so let me share this truth and may you receive it from my heart to yours. True love lays down their life for another.

True love is kind, patient and does not bring harm, but wants to help. True love would rather make things right, than be right. True love, when put to the test, is proven through trials and trust. True love can only be seen in the relationship when conflict comes and a decision is made to walk away or fight for the relationship. This is why I ask you to guard your heart until you know who you're giving it away to. I don't want my daughter to give the most valuable thing you have to someone who will throw it away and make you feel worthless. You, my beloved, are worthy of love. If you feel you have to prove your worth, that is a warning you must pay attention to. Seek me with all your heart and your heart will stay safe. Make me your first love and you will never have to compromise again. I will bring those who will love you the way that you deserve to be loved as my daughter if you will make me your number one. Anyone that I send you will draw you closer to me and complete the calling I have on your life.

Love
Your Father in Heaven

"Love is patient, love is kind. It does not envy, it does not boast, it is not proud. It does not dishonor others, it is not self-seeking, it is not easily angered, it keeps no record of wrongs."
1 Corinthians 13:4-5

Royal Reflection

How do you feel about yourself after you spent time with the friends you have chosen?

Royal Reflection

Royal Reflection

The Garden of Grief

My Beloved Princess,

I see you when you are in the garden of grief. I hear your cry for help in the dark hours of the night. When you hurt, I hurt and it breaks My heart to watch you cry without Me. I am here with you desiring to be the shoulder your tears fall on. I Myself cried out in the garden the night I was betrayed. In My suffering I asked My Father for another way—a less painful way. Yet I trusted His will and purpose for My life.

I knew the ultimate victory was at the cross. Just as olives must be crushed to make oil, I poured out My life as a love offering for you. Don't ever doubt that I am with you, and that I long to take you to a place of comfort, peace, and victory. Even when you cannot see Me from where you are, I am working on your behalf. Give to Me the crushing weight of your circumstances, and come to Me in prayer. When it is time to leave the garden, I will walk with you across the valley and straight to the cross—where your trials will be transformed into triumph.

Love,
Your Savior and your key to freedom

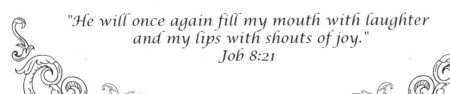

"He will once again fill my mouth with laughter
and my lips with shouts of joy."
Job 8:21

Royal Reflection

There's a difference between a better heart and a broken heart. Just because you're hurting, doesn't mean you haven't forgiven someone that hurt you.

Royal Reflection

Royal Reflection

My Precious Child,

I want you to have a passion in your heart for Me and My written Word. I promise you, the more you read My Word, the more you will want Me. Don't let anyone or anything steal that time away from you and Me. I know you love Me, but I often find you looking everywhere else except to Me. It's My Word that lets you live life with supernatural wisdom. It's My Word that defines who you are and how much I love you. I know there is much to see and do, but nothing will give you the blessings or security that you will discover in the love letter I've written for you—My Word.

Open your Bible today, and let Me reveal Myself to you in a very real and intimate way. Any time you spend with Me will be multiplied by My mighty hand, so draw near to Me and I will draw near to you.

Love,
Your Living Word

"Your commandments give me understanding; no wonder I hate every false way of life. Your word is a lamp to guide my feet and a light for my path."
Psalm 119:104-105

Royal Reflection

We will not experience...
Peace without trust,
Power without prayer,
Victory without accountability,
Wisdom without reading the Word.

Royal Reflection

Royal Reflection

My Appointed Princess,

Just as there are seasons throughout the year, your life is seasonal as well. In each season you clothe yourself differently and you do different activities, weather permitting. The same is true with your life, my love. You must learn to submit to each new season so you can step into your next appointed position. I know you long to settle into a season once and for all. However, that is not how life works until you are home with me.

For now I need you to represent me wherever you are to the very best of your ability. Your life will have meaning and your legacy will live on forever if you will submit to each season. Your appointed position is not just for you, it's for my kingdom work . You are the daughter of the king and being a part of a royal family comes with responsibility and privilege. I've given you one life to live on earth and eternity to celebrate what you've done while you're here.

If you waste your life living in the past or your future, you will find discontentment and discouragement. I'm asking you as my daughter to step into the place you're most effective. It is in that place that my grace has gone before you and my joy is waiting to become your strength.

Love,
Your King forever

"For everything there is a season,
a time for every activity under heaven."
Ecclesiastes 3:1

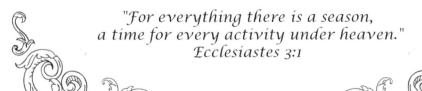

Royal Reflection

*God's timing is just as important as
God's will for our lives.*

_____
_____
_____
_____
_____
_____
_____
_____
_____
_____
_____
_____
_____
_____
_____
_____
_____
_____
_____
_____
_____
_____
_____
_____
_____
_____
_____
_____
_____
_____
_____

Royal Reflection

Royal Reflection

Life's Not Fair Yet

My Beloved Daughter,

My heart breaks—just like yours does as I watch how the people I created treat one another. I warned you in My Word that there will be suffering here on earth, but I have overcome this world. Don't look to people to find Me. The power to persevere through trials cannot be found in this world. Instead, look up, and I will give you an eternal perspective and new hope. I know life is not fair yet, when I return for you, My beloved, I will wipe away every tear.

All pain and suffering will come to an end. But for now I want you to be a light of My love to this dark world. I want you to find joy in knowing that I am coming to your rescue. For now, however, find strength in knowing that every choice you make to walk by faith and not by sight will enable you to rise above others' actions or reactions. You will find My peace by choosing to live in light of eternity from this day forward.

Love,
Your Heavenly Daddy

"I have told you all this so that you may
have peace in Me. Here on earth you
will have many trials and sorrows.
But take heart, because
I have overcome the world."
John 16:33

Royal Reflection

Place your hurts and offenses in the hands of your loving father in heaven. May you listen to His still voice whisper, "Trust Me."

Royal Reflection

Royal Reflection

The Bait of Anger

My Warrior Daughter,

I know there is much happening in the world to get angry about. However, anger is a trap set by the enemy for your soul. If you take the bait of anger you will become bitter. Nothing good is ever birthed out of bitterness, My beloved.

So, when you feel angry, cry out to Me and confess that anger. I am the One who can handle your heart and walk you through the battlefields of rage and anger. I will teach you how to live a life free from the destruction anger brings. You can be at peace as you learn to trust Me to deal with all those who have hurt My girl.

Love,
Your King Who Is Just

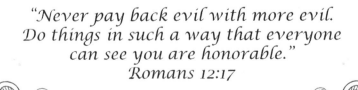

"Never pay back evil with more evil.
Do things in such a way that everyone
can see you are honorable."
Romans 12:17

Royal Reflection

*Peace takes training. When you're in Boot Camp
you train for war so you won't crumble
when the battle hits.*

Royal Reflection

Royal Reflection

My Dear Princess,

You need not worry when your life will end. All you need to know is that your first breath began with Me, and your last breath will lead you to My presence. Don't ever let fear of death or eternity frighten you. Your todays and tomorrows are secure with Me—I have held them in My hand since the beginning of time. When you finish your brief time on earth and I call you into My presence, your forever life in heaven will begin. But for now, My chosen one, you must live free from fear.

Instead, trust Me to take you through every trial that comes your way. Remember that nothing in the universe can separate us. I am with you always...Even until the end of time. So live well and finish strong—fixing your hope on the day that we will meet face-to-face on the other side of eternity.

Love,
Your Eternal King

"He said to me: "It is done. I am the Alpha and the Omega, the Beginning and the End. To the thirsty I will give water without cost from the spring of the water of life."
Revelation 21:6

Royal Reflection

"If we find ourselves with a desire that nothing in the world can satisfy, the most probable explanation is that we were made for another world."
-C.S. Lewis

Royal Reflection

Royal Reflection

My Princess,

I know many days you feel like a weary warrior, too tired to fight. I see you when you have exhausted your faith and lost your passion for My people. Today, I want to paint an eternal picture for My beloved warrior. Every act of kindness you share will water someone's thirsty soul. Every time you pray for someone, you are changing their destiny from darkness to light.

You are more than a light in the darkness. Your faith will continue to be a raging fire that will burn in the hearts of many generations who follow your wonderful works on earth!

Love,
Your Forever King

"They share freely and give generously to those in need. Their good deeds will be remembered forever. They will have influence and honor."
Psalm 112:9

Royal Reflection

May you grasp how truly valueable you are in the eternal picture of life. I pray for the joy of heaven to reign in your heart all the rest of your days.

Royal Reflection

Royal Reflection

My Beloved,

I want to reveal a sacred secret to you. Although I am your God, I am also your eternal Husband. I will come soon to carry you over the threshold into eternity. My desire is to lift the veil from your eyes that you might see who you really are, My Princess, My Bride.

I am the lover of your soul. I long to get close enough to give you a glimpse of my eternal love for you. One day, there will be a glorious celebration and we will see each other face-to-face. On that day, you will realize that your life is finally complete and your joy more full than you could ever dream possible. Every negative emotion loosed on you in this life will depart forever. Every pain that has burrowed its way into your soul will disappear forever. Then I will gently wipe away the last tear from your cheek and embrace you beloved and say, "You will never cry again, My love... Welcome Home."

Love,
Your King and your Bridegroom

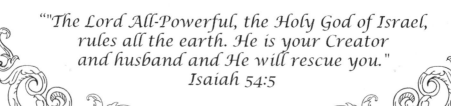

""The Lord All-Powerful, the Holy God of Israel, rules all the earth. He is your Creator and husband and He will rescue you."
Isaiah 54:5

Royal Reflection
Wedding Vows to My God

My God, My Groom

Today I say "I Do." I will take, My Eternal, loving
Husband what I know of You, and trusting what I
do not yet know
I take you for better or for worse,
For richer or for poorer,
In times of sickness and in times of health,
In times of joy and in times of sorrow,
In times of failure and in times of triumph,

In times of plenty and in times of want,
To have and to hold from this day forward
until death places me in Your arms.

Love your Princess Bride
Who says, "I do!"

"I saw the Holy City, the New Jerusalem, coming
down out of heaven from God, prepared as a bride
beautifully dressed for her husband. And I heard a
loud voice from the throne saying, 'Now the
dwelling of God is with men, and he will live with
them. They will be his people, and God himself will
be with them and be their God. He will wipe every
tear from their eyes. There will be no more death
or mourning or crying or pain, for the old order of
things has passed away.' He who is seated on the
thrown will make all things new. Write these
things down for these words are trustworthy and
true."
Revelation 21:2-4

Royal Reflection

Royal Reflection

My Princess Warrior,

When you are too weak to fight, simply stand. When the spiritual warfare around you becomes great and you are in the heat of a faith battle and don't know what to do, I want you to stand! Stand on My promises. Stand for what you know to be right! Stand in the gap for those who can't stand on their own!

Yes, My love, evil days will come, but you have My Spirit inside you, and in My power you can and will stand! It is your confidence in Me that will give others the strength to stand with you. Once you have done everything you can, you will still be standing!

Love,
Your King Who Stands In For You

"So put on all of God's armor. Evil days will come.
But you will be able to stand up to anything.
And after you have done everything you can,
you will still be standing."
Ephesians 6:13

Royal Reflection

You will be victorious over every evil thing that comes against you, and you will not stay down. You were designed to be a conqueror and to finish strong!

Royal Reflection

Royal Reflection

My Beautiful Daughter,

Your legacy means so much more than the life you wanted. I will make you a hero of the faith if you choose to live for Me. Every tough choice you make to obey Me will become a foundation of faith for your family. Your commitment to My call will carve character in the next generation. Every prayer you pray will become a blessing passed down. Your courage will continue to bring comfort to many during their difficult times. Your trust in Me will remain in others who watched you walk in peace.

I, your God, declare on this day that your children's children will be forever blessed because you lived your life for an audience of one: Me!

Love,
Your Heavenly Father

"I lavish my love on those who love me
and obey my commands,
even for a thousand generations."
Exodus 20:6

Royal Reflection

May you find so much meaning in knowing your decision to live driven by eternity will break generational curses and start a new foundation of blessings!

Royal Reflection

Royal Reflection

It is Finished!

My Warrior Daughter,

It is finished, My beloved Princess. I, your Savior, paid the price for your eternal life when I drew My last breath on the cross. I conquered death, I covered your sin with My blood, and I loved you with My life. Now My Spirit is in you to finish the work you have been sent to do. My Power is yours to use. My keys to freedom are now yours to share. My grace is your gift to receive.

All regret or guilt is gone and new life has come, because it is finished. If you ever begin to doubt how much you are loved, look at the cross. It is finished, and you will finish strong!

Love,
Your Lord Who Paid It All For You!

"For it is by grace you have been saved,
through faith - and this is not from yourselves,
it is the gift of God - not by works,
so no one can boast."
Ephesians 2:8-9

Royal Reflection

Yes, it is a spiritual fight to live for God, but there is no adventure on earth that is more exciting or everlasting than serving the King of kings.

Royal Reflection

Royal Reflection

Precious Princess,

I pray as you have read through these letters, you have discovered that God's love, power, and promises are for you. But I could not let you finish without making sure you know the King of Kings our Heavenly Father personally. Reading about God's love is not enough to secure a place in His eternal kingdom. He invites us to accept His everlasting invitation and receive the gift of His Son Jesus Christ as our Lord and Savior . I would love the privilege of being a part of your eternal crowning by asking you to say this simple prayer with me:

Dear God, I don't want to live without You any longer. I believe You sent Your Son to die for me and I want Him to be my Lord and my King. I confess my sin and my need for a Savior. I accept Your free gift of everlasting life. I thank You for writing my name in Your book of life.
I pray this prayer by faith in Jesus' name. Amen!

If this is your sincere prayer, you can know that angels are rejoicing and the Holy Spirit of the Living God is now in you. If I don't have the honor of meeting you during your reign through this life, I look forward to celebrating with you on the other side of eternity. Until then, may our our Daddy bless your walk with Him.

Love your sister in Christ,
Sheri Rose

"I tell you the truth, whoever hears My Word and believes Him who sent Me has eternal life and will not be condemned; he has crossed over from death to life."
John 5:24

For more journals, books, online coaching, or to attend or book a conference with Sheri Rose Shepherd, be sure to visit her or email her personally at:

Website:
HisRoyalFamily.com

Email:
rose@hisprincess.com

Made in the USA
Coppell, TX
12 May 2020